ADAPTATION FOR SURVIVAL

SKIN

WRITTEN BY STEPHEN SAVAGE

Thomson Learning
New York

ADAPTATION FOR SURVIVAL

Books in the series

• EYES • EARS • HANDS AND FEET
• MOUTHS • NOSES • SKIN

Front cover: Girls with rabbits, a chameleon

Title page: A leopard

First published in the United States in 1995 by
Thomson Learning
New York, NY

Published simultaneously in Great Britain by Wayland (Publishers) Limited

U.S. version copyright © 1995 Thomson Learning

U.K. version copyright © 1995 Wayland (Publishers) Limited

Library of Congress Cataloging-in-Publication
Savage, Stephen, 1965–
   Skin / written by Stephen Savage.
     p.   cm.—(Adaptation for survival)
   Includes bibliographical references and index.
   Summary: Describes the body coverings of humans and other animals,
explaining the varying uses of skin, fur, feathers, spines, scales, and hair.
   ISBN 1-56847-353-2 (hc)
   1. Skin—Juvenile literature. 2. Body covering (Anatomy)—Juvenile
literature. [1. Body covering (Anatomy) 2. Skin. 3. Animal defenses.] I. Title.
II. Series: Savage, Stephen, 1965– Adaptation for survival.
QL941.S28   1995
591.1'858—dc20   95-19239

Printed in Italy

Picture acknowledgments
The publishers would like to thank the following for allowing their photographs to be reproduced in this book: Bruce
Coleman Limited: 7 (top/Gerald Cubitt) (bottom/Jeff Foott), 9 (Hans Reinhard), 10 (Kim Taylor), 12 (bottom/Gary
Retherford), 13 (top/Frans Lanting), 14 (Jane Burton), 15 (top/John Cancalosi) (bottom/Jane Burton), 18 (bottom/John
Cancalosi), 19 (top/Jane Burton) (bottom/Andrew J. Purcell), 23 (top/Erwin & Peggy Bauer), 24 (bottom/Hector
Rivarola), 25 (top/Luiz Claudio Marigo) (bottom/M. P. L. Fogden), 26 (bottom/Brian J. Coates), 28 (bottom/Jane
Burton), 29 (Kim Taylor); Cephas: 18 (top/Dorothy Burrows); Natural History Photographic Agency: *cover*
(bottom/Gerard Lacz), 16 (Anthony Bannister), 21 (bottom/Jenry Ausloos), 23 (bottom/Stephen Dalton); Oxford
Scientific Films: *title page* (David W. Breed), 4 (top/G I Bernard), 8 (Michael Leach), 11 (top/James H. Robinson)
(bottom/Stan Osolinski), 12 (top/Z. Leszcynski), 13 (bottom/Max Gibbs), 17 (top/Howard Hall) (bottom/Pam & Willy
Kemp), 20 (Doug Allan), 21 (top/David B. Fleetham), 24 (top/Leonard Lee Rue), 26 (top/Andrew Plumptre), 28 (top/Zig
Lesczynski); Tony Stone Worldwide: 5 (top/Sue Ann Miller); Wayland: *cover* (top), 5 (bottom), 27 (top); ZEFA: 6
(Liedermooy), 22 (Will & Demi McIntyre), 27 (bottom/John Flowerdew). The artwork on pages 4 and 31 is by Peter Bull.

Contents

Human Skin

One square centimeter (.155 square inch) of human skin contains approximately ten hairs, three feet of blood vessels, one hundred sweat glands, and millions of skin cells. It also contains numerous sense cells that send messages to the brain about the things that it touches.

The human body is completely covered by skin. This skin is made up of many layers of skin cells and is the body's largest organ. The top layer of skin is made from dead cells and helps protect the body from dirt and harmful bacteria.

A layer of cells near the surface of the skin reacts to the harmful rays of the sun by producing a protective pigment (color). Pigment can cause skin to form freckles or if someone stays out in the sun for too long, to sunburn. Sunburned skin is red and sore.

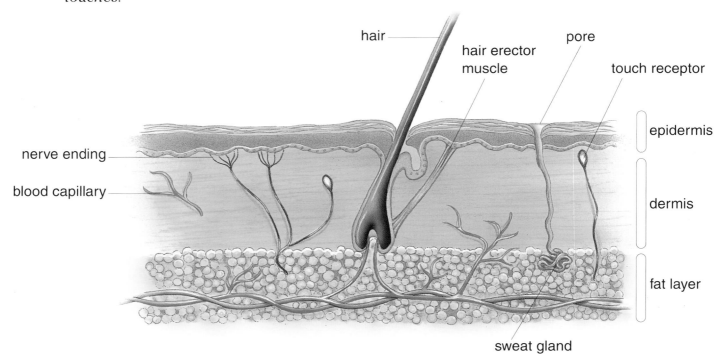

A baby's skin is soft and flexible. As people get older, their skin becomes drier and less elastic, causing it to wrinkle.

Sunburned skin is damaged and will peel off after a few days. People who get sunburned often may permanently damage their skin. The sun is at its strongest at the equator. People living in the areas of the world nearest to the equator (or those whose ancestors did) have dark skin. This adaptation partly protects them from the harmful rays of the sun.

The skin is also a sense organ for touch. There are many special cells in the skin. Some are sensitive to cold, heat, or pain. Some skin is slightly different in its structure: hair and nails. As will be shown in this book, a fish's scales, a cat's fur, a bird's feathers, and a tortoise's shell are also special skin cells.

Human skin contains sense cells that enable the whole body to feel. This boy is enjoying the softness of the rabbit's fur against his skin.

Thick Skin

Human skin is very thin and easily damaged. If people cut or graze themselves, special pain cells send the message that the skin is damaged and need treatment. The damaged area can be covered with a bandage to keep dirt and bacteria from getting into the wound while new skin cells grow.

Some animals, such as rhinoceroses and elephants, have very thick skin. This protects them against injury from predators and other animals of the same species. The skin of an elephant can be over an inch thick on some parts of its body.

Even a thick-skinned elephant can find a mosquito bite troublesome. This one is trying to protect its skin from bites by covering itself in mud.

The horn of the rhinoceros is actually made from a special type of skin. The cells are so tightly packed that the horn is extremely hard. The rhinoceros uses its horn to defend itself from predators and in fights with other rhinos.

Seals and sea lions come ashore on beaches to have their pups. A male seal or sea lion will defend an area of beach from other males by fighting them off. They use their sharp teeth as weapons, biting each other's necks, if they get the chance. The skin and fat (blubber) around their necks is much thicker than on other parts of the body. This means that they rarely do any serious damage to one another.

The thick layer of skin and blubber (fat) around this male sea lion's neck protects it from bites in battles with other sea lions.

Hair and Fur

Although all mammals are covered in skin, most are also covered in hair or fur for extra protection. Animals that are covered in hair include horses, monkeys, and pigs. Humans are covered with hair follicles, but human hair varies in thickness and length depending on the part of the body on which it appears. Only a few places, such as the palms of human hands, are totally hairless.

Other animals, such as cats of all sizes, rabbits, and mice, are covered in fur. Fur is similar to hair, but much finer and softer. Both hair and fur keep animals warm. Only humans need to wear clothing for warmth.

A chinchilla has perhaps the softest fur of all mammals.

Some of the clothes people wear are made from the hair of animals. Sheep, for example, have thick, hairy coats that can be cut off and turned into yarn. This is done by a process called spinning. Yarn is used to make all kinds of clothes and blankets.

An animal's hair or fur changes throughout its life. Most furry or hairy animals will change their coats according to the season, growing thicker coats for the winter and shedding them in the spring.

Some animals, including cats, mice, and moles, have thick hairs, called whiskers, on their heads and faces. The whiskers are connected at their roots to sensitive cells, so the animals can feel if the whiskers touch anything. Whiskers are very useful when animals are finding their way around in the dark.

Some mammals, such as mice, squirrels, and rabbits, are born bald and grow fur after a few days. This mother rabbit has pulled out some of her own fur to keep her newborn babies warm.

Feathers

The body of a bird is covered in feathers. Like hair and fur, this body covering grows from the skin and helps keep the bird warm. The feathers that give each bird its typical shape are called contour feathers. Underneath these is a layer of soft, downy feathers. Female ducks actually pull out some of these feathers to line their nests. Baby birds often have downy feathers before their adult feathers grow.

A bird's feathers must be kept in good condition, and much of the bird's time is taken up with preening and bathing. Birds regularly change all their feathers (molt) every so often.

The feathers on a bird's wings are called flight feathers. These allow birds to travel great distances to find food or escape from danger. The owl has very soft flight feathers, so it can silently swoop down on its prey. A bird's tail feathers are used to help it balance when flying or sitting on a branch.

Birds use their feathers to blend in with their surroundings. The female mallard duck, for example, is a dull brown so that she can sit on her nest and not be seen. Birds also use their feathers to give out signals to other birds —either to attract them or to warn them away.

▲ *The cormorant's feathers are not waterproof and tend to become waterlogged when it swims. This makes the cormorant heavy in the water, so it can stay beneath the surface for a long time, searching for fish. It spends a lot of time drying itself in the sun and wind.*

The feathers of a penguin (and of many other waterbirds) are waterproof. This means that they do not absorb water. In fact, the penguin's feathers trap a layer of air next to the body, which helps the bird bob back up to the surface after diving for fish.

Scales

Many creatures are covered in scales. Scales can be large and thick enough to protect the animal against attack or so small that the animal feels smooth and soft to the touch. Some lizards have hard and spiky skin, while others have softer skin like that of a snake. Many people think that snakes are cold and slimy, but in fact a snake's skin is warm and dry. Snakes move by pushing themselves along the ground with the large scales on the undersides of their bodies.

▲ *If a snake were smooth all over, it would be very difficult for it to move along. The large scales on its underside help it push itself along the ground.*

Scales can be found in surprising places. The colored patterns on a butterfly's wings are made from thousands of tiny scales.

The shell of this giant tortoise is actually made from extremely hard skin cells.

Animals that use their scales for protection include the tortoise, whose body is covered in hard scales that form a shell. Its legs and head are covered in tough, scaly skin, like that on crocodiles and alligators.

The bodies of most types of fish are covered in protective scales. Fish feel slimy because of a special thick mucus that covers their bodies. This helps them glide through the water and also helps protect them from infection. Like mammals and birds, the color and pattern on their body covering can be used for camouflage or for display.

The scales on the body of this cichlid overlap like tiles on a roof.

Spiny Bodies

Spikes and spines are good ways to protect the body. Hedgehogs and porcupines use their sharp spines to defend themselves against attack. When approached by an attacker, the porcupine sticks up the spines on its back and tail. If this does not frighten away its attacker, the porcupine rushes backward, ramming its spikes, or quills, into its enemy. When threatened, the European hedgehog curls itself into a tight, prickly ball.

The European hedgehog rolls itself into a tight ball to keep predators away. This one, feeling itself to be out of danger, is just beginning to unroll.

When threatened, the Australian echidna sticks up its sharp spines.

When it feels itself to be in danger, a porcupine fish blows itself up. This causes its spikes (which usually lie flat against its body) to stick out and makes it an unappetizing mouthful.

Sea urchins belong to a group of animals called echinoderms, which means spiny-skinned. The sea urchin's body is covered in long spines that protect these slow-moving animals. The spines of some types of sea urchins are poisonous.

Many fish have spines on their fins and gill covers, but some fish have other defensive spines. The three-spined stickleback has spines on its back that the fish sticks up when attacked, making it hard for other fish to swallow.

Living Shells

This giant African land snail is the largest shelled mollusk on land.

Another way of protecting the body is to live inside a hard shell. There are many animals, called mollusks, that do this. Some have single shells (such as snails); others have shells made up of two halves (such as mussels). Unlike the shell of a tortoise, the shells of animals such as snails and mussels are not made from skin cells. They are formed by a thick liquid that oozes out of the animal's body and then hardens.

Animals with one shell are able to move around by carrying their shells on their backs. Only a few live on land, the largest being the giant African land snail. Most snails live in ponds, rivers, or oceans.

The shells of sea snails may be spiral, smooth, or spiky, and some are brightly colored. Many, like the winkle, feed by scraping tiny seaweeds and algae off rocks. Others, such as the dog whelk, can actually attack and eat a mussel by drilling a hole through its shell.

There are many creatures that have two halves to their shells. These tend to stay in one place, absorbing food from their surroundings, but most are able to move a short distance to escape from danger or find a better place to feed. Mussels attach themselves to rocks using sticky threads. Piddocks actually bore into rocks for extra protection. Oysters and scallops lie on the seabed, while razor clams hide beneath the sand.

▲ *The giant clam can grow to a size of four feet across and can weigh four hundred pounds.*

Seashells, like this cowrie, have been used as ornaments and for jewelry. On some Pacific islands, cowrie shells have even been used as money.

Armor

Humans have used artificial ways of protecting their soft skin when fighting. Suits of armor like these were worn hundreds of years ago. The overlapping plates on the arms are similar to those on the body of the armadillo.

A shell provides good protection against predators, but it makes it difficult to move around. Some animals, such as insects, spiders, crabs, and lobsters, have armored bodies instead. The armor consists of a tough skin that is jointed, allowing the animal to walk or run. In fact, these animals have no bones under their flesh. This outer shell is more than just a body covering; it is a kind of outside skeleton.

Safe inside its protective armor, a crab can move around in search of food or to avoid danger. Crabs have large, armored pincers that they use when feeding or when defending themselves.

A nine-banded armadillo. The narrow overlapping bands of armor make it more flexible than a tortoise, with its rigid shell, is.

The hermit crab has armored skin only on its limbs and part of its body. It protects the rest of its body with an empty seashell, which it moves into and carries around on its back. This land hermit crab lives in Southeast Asia.

The crab's shell often blends in with its surroundings, as is the case with the adult shore crab, which has a green body for hiding in seaweed-covered tidal pools. Spider crabs have hooks on their backs onto which they attach seaweed.

Insects have firm outer skins that support and protect their bodies. Although the skin is not as tough as a crab's, it does help protect them against attack from other small creatures. Some beetles have hard, shiny wing cases that look something like shells.

Like other beetles, the ladybug has hard wing cases that cover most of its body.

Water Mammals

Although human skin is waterproof, we are not really adapted to live in the water. A major problem to overcome is how to keep warm. People get cold in the water, even in a heated swimming pool. This is because the water takes away body heat. People who spend a long time in cold water, such as divers and windsurfers, wear wet suits to keep themselves warm.

Many types of whales feed in cold, polar seas, then travel to warmer waters each year to give birth. Some of the mother whale's blubber is turned into milk to feed her calf. The baby whale must develop a thick layer of blubber in order to survive when it returns to colder water with its mother.

The Weddell seal lives in the Antarctic, where temperatures on land may be colder than -5°F. The seal dives underneath the ice to escape from the winter gales. At such times it will be warmer in the water than on the land.

An otter's water-repellent fur helps keep it warm both in the water and on land.

Mammals that live in cold water, such as whales and dolphins, have developed a kind of body fat called blubber. The blubber of a large whale may be up to two feet thick in some places. A blue whale can weigh 160 tons. Just over a third of this weight may be its skin and blubber. Some types of whales migrate from their feeding grounds to warmer areas to breed. For several months each year they do not eat, and their body fat turns into energy.

Seals and sea lions also have blubber to protect them against the cold. Their bodies are covered in hair because, unlike dolphins and whales, they spend some time on land. The otter, on the other hand, hardly has any blubber and relies on its thick coat of fur to keep it warm.

Keeping Warm or Cool

Humans can survive in cold climates because they live in heated homes and wear special clothing. In the winter people can wrap up to keep warm. Explorers can survive even in the frozen polar regions or in the freezing cold of space. People avoid overheating in the summer or in hot climates by wearing the right clothes. Light-colored clothes are best when the sun is strong, because they reflect the heat. Dark-colored clothes absorb heat.

Whatever the temperature of the air, the human internal body temperature tends to remain around the same (about 98.6°F) unless the person is sick.

This Arab boy is wearing clothes suitable for a hot climate. The long sleeves and headdress protect his skin from the sun's rays, and the white fabric reflects the heat.

The body temperature of some animals, however, depends entirely on the temperature of their surroundings. These are called cold-blooded animals, and they include reptiles. First thing in the morning, the crocodile can only move very slowly, but as its body takes in warmth from the sun and its blood warms up, it becomes more active and can move more quickly. When it gets too hot it will cool off in the water.

People who live in freezing climates have traditionally worn animal skins to keep warm.

Some insects and spiders can actually survive the cold winter asleep because of a chemical in their blood that keeps them from freezing. Fish that live in the cold polar seas survive in the same way. Many mammals escape the cold by hibernating—finding a warm dry place and going into a deep sleep that can last through the entire winter.

A chameleon turns a dark color to get warm by absorbing the heat of the sun. If it becomes too hot, the chameleon turns a light color, which reflects the heat. This one is just beginning to turn a light green.

Hiding from Danger

The large, light-colored spots on the dark back of this fawn look like the patterns of light and shade made in forests. The spots make the deer less likely to be seen by predators.

The patterns and colors on many types of animals have adapted to blend in with the animal's surroundings. The right color and pattern can completely camouflage an animal. The sandy-brown fur of a lion helps it to stalk its prey across the sandy-brown earth and grass of the African plains. Animals that live in the Arctic, such as the polar bear and Arctic fox, are white, so they don't show up against the snow. The ptarmigan, a bird found in areas that are snow-covered only in winter, changes its feathers from brown in the summer to white in the winter.

This stick insect is so well camouflaged it looks almost more like a stick than the stick does!

Insects are particularly good at blending in with their surroundings. The many different kinds of stick insects have all adapted to look like the plants on which they feed. Some insects do very convincing imitations of twigs, leaves, and tree bark. The looper caterpillar, or inchworm, looks like a plant stem, while the bush cricket mimics a dead leaf. The umber moth is almost invisible on tree bark, and the Chinese character moth looks like a distasteful bird dropping.

Some creatures take the business of camouflage a step further and actually change color from moment to moment, depending on where they are. The chameleon is the best known of these. It can change from green to brown in a matter of minutes as it moves from a leaf to a tree trunk. Flatfish and octopuses can change the colors of their bodies to match the seabed by expanding and contracting special skin cells that make different colors appear.

This Brazilian butterfly mimics a dead leaf, including imitation spots of black and white mold.

A leaf frog, almost completely hidden on the forest floor

Showing Off

The silver fur of this mountain gorilla shows that he is the leader of his group.

▼ *The magnificent male bird of paradise is about to display his tail feathers to attract a female.*

Many animals use their body coverings for display, to send signals to other animals. The fur on the back of a dog's neck will stand up when it is angry, and the fur on a cat's tail will do the same. Monkeys raise and lower their eyebrows to communicate anger and alarm to other monkeys.

Many birds, normally the males, have developed brightly colored feathers. These are used both to attract females and to frighten off competitors. Females are usually a dull color, so they blend in with their surroundings when sitting on their nests. Parrots may stick up their head feathers to form a threatening display.

This traditional clown make-up makes the child's eyes, lips, and cheeks look much bigger than they really are. When worn by a professional clown in a circus ring, the make-up enables the clown's face and expressions to be seen even from the back row of seats.

▼ *A Masai warrior in traditional dress, with skin originally painted to frighten the enemy*

The color of human skin reddens when a person is embarrassed, hot, or angry, but humans have no control over this. People cannot change the color of their skin. Instead, people all over the world paint their bodies and faces. The way in which they do this varies and depends on what is considered beautiful or fierce in the society in which they live.

Skin Change

An American corn snake shedding its skin. When a snake needs to renew its skin, a lubricating liquid is released under the skin. This separates the old skin from the new skin underneath, turning the old skin cloudy—even where it covers the snake's eyes. The snake, unable to see well, will hide away for up to a week until the skin is ready to be shed. The snake then will wriggle out of its old skin in a matter of minutes.

When animals are molting they tend to look somewhat scruffy.

Throughout our lives we shed thousands of tiny dead skin cells, which are replaced by new ones. Some animals shed whole layers of skin at one time. Snakes and lizards shed their skin in this way, and underneath the old skin is a new, shiny skin.

Birds molt their feathers a few at a time, so they always have enough to fly with and to keep them warm. Mammals molt their fur or hair at certain times of the year. A thick coat of fur that has kept an animal warm all winter will not be needed in the summer. When a pet dog or cat molts in the spring it leaves hairs all over the furniture.

Most insects, including butterflies and dragonflies, change their shapes several times before they become adults. These changes are called metamorphoses.

This dragonfly has just climbed out of its old, nymphal, skin (which it is leaving behind, still clinging to a stalk) and has now changed into an adult dragonfly.

Crabs have to shed their old armored shells so that they can grow. They swell their bodies with water, which splits the old shell. The crab then climbs out of its armor. The skin underneath is soft, so it must hide away from danger until the shell hardens. Locusts, wood lice, and spiders also shed their tough skins as they grow.

Glossary

Absorb Take in water or heat.

Algae Very small plants that grow in water but have no stems, roots, or leaves.

Ancestors Relatives who lived a long time ago.

Bacteria Tiny living creatures that can cause infection or illness.

Blubber A thick layer of body fat in animals such as whales and seals that helps keep them warm.

Camouflage To hide by having a body that is the same color or shape as the surrounding area (grass, sand, etc.).

Cell The smallest structure of living matter.

Contract Get smaller or close up.

Expand Get larger or open up.

Hibernate Spend the winter in a deep sleep.

Lubricating liquid A slippery liquid, like an oil.

Migrate Journey between two areas at certain times of the year, usually to avoid very bad weather, to find food, or to have offspring.

Molt To shed body covering (such as skin, feathers, or shell) so that it can be replaced by a new one.

Mucus A protective slime.

Predator An animal that kills other animals for food.

Prey An animal that is hunted for food.

Reflect Cause light and heat to bounce off.

Shed Get rid of.

Sweat A salty liquid that comes out of holes in the skin in hot weather to help cool the body down.

Further Reading

Bennett, Paul. *Changing Shape.* Nature's Secrets. New York: Thomson Learning, 1994.

O'Connor, Karen. *The Feather Book.* New York: Dillon Press, 1990.

Parker, Steve. *Touching a Nerve: How You Touch, Sense and Feel.* The Body in Action. New York: Franklin Watts, 1992.

Ward, Brian. *Skin: And Its Care.* Health Guides. New York: Franklin Watts, 1990.

Further Notes

The human body is completely covered with skin, which protects the internal organs from the surrounding environment. It protects the body from internal injury, the sun's harmful rays, and infection from bacteria. Skin helps control the body's temperature and acts as a sensory organ, giving humans a sense of touch and enabling them to detect cold, heat, and pain.

Keeping warm or cool

Blood capillaries near the surface of the skin can help prevent the body from becoming too hot. The capillaries widen, allowing more hot blood to flow near the skin's surface and therefore more heat to be lost. When it is cold the capillaries become smaller, reducing the amount of blood that flows near the surface and the amount of heat lost. Although the outer skin temperature may vary greatly, the internal body temperature of a healthy person stays fairly constant at between 97.8°F and 99°F.

Sweating also helps to cool the body temperature. When body temperature rises, the sweat glands absorb water from the surrounding capillaries. The water collects in the glands and eventually travels up the sweat duct and onto the skin. As the sweat evaporates, it takes heat from the body and helps cool it down.

Parts of the human skin

Epidermis – Tough outer layer of skin cells that forms a protective layer. The surface of human skin is made up of dead skin cells.

Dermis – This layer contains blood vessels, sweat glands, and nerves with sensors to detect heat, cold, pain, and texture.

Follicle – A hole in the skin out of which a hair grows.

Malpighian layer -- This layer produces skin pigment that protects the body against the sun's rays.

Sensory nerves – Separate sensory nerves can detect cold, pain, heat, and texture.

Blood capillaries – These bring oxygen and food to the skin and remove carbon dioxide. The capillaries close to the surface of the skin help control body temperature.

Sweat glands – These produce sweat (salty water) that passes on to the surface of the skin through a pore (hole) when the body is hot.

Erector muscles – These make hairs on the skin stand up.

Fat layer – This is a food store that can be broken down by the body and used if necessary. It also forms an insulating layer to reduce heat loss from the body.

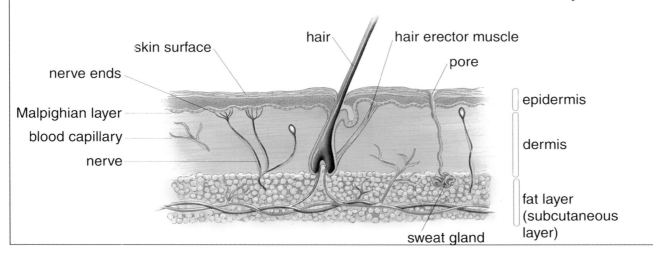

Index